TRACK & FIELD

WARMING UP

by Dan Zadra

Published by
The Children's Book Company
Mankato, Minnesota

Text/Design/Photography
by James Rothaus & Associates

Editor: Dan Zadra, Editor-In-Chief, YOUNG ATHLETE Magazine.
Bob Honey and Linda Carey, Design and Production.
Tom Horton, Photography.

Published by The Children's Book Company, P.O. Box 113,
Mankato, Minnesota 56001

Library of Congress Number: 81-67700

ISBN: 0-89813-014-X

HOW JESSE OWENS LEARNED A GREAT TRACK AND FIELD SECRET FROM THE KING OF BEASTS

Jesse Owens was one of the greatest track stars the world has ever seen. For almost a decade, Jesse was known throughout the world as the fastest man alive.

At the 1936 Olympic Games in Berlin, Germany, Jesse took on the best athletes Adolph Hitler could set against him. And each time Jesse came out victorious for America.

After the Olympics, Jesse traveled to country fairs in towns and cities across our nation. There, he would amaze the crowds by defeating their swiftest thoroughbred horses in 100-yard foot races.

One day a young farm boy was watching Jesse get ready to race a very fast horse from a famous local stable. The young lad scratched his head in wonder as Jesse slowly stretched

3

Jesse Owens

4

his legs and arms. Over and over Jesse would bend at the waist to touch his toes, or reach high in the air to stretch the rippling muscles of his upper arms and back. Finally, the young boy's curiosity got the best of him.

"Excuse me, Mr. Owens," he almost whispered. "Could you please tell me what that stretchin' is all about?"

Jesse looked up and grinned. Slowly, he walked over to the boy, knelt down and looked him in the eye.

"Son," said Jesse with a smile, "have you ever seen a lion in a zoo?"

"Yes sir," answered the boy.

"Well, then," said Jesse, "you've probably noticed that lions love to stretch. It's one of their favorite things to do, and they do it for a reason.

"You see, son," Jesse continued, "lions learned thousands of years ago that stretching keeps their muscles strong and loose. If a lion didn't stretch, his legs would be too tight to run across the plains after antelope. Stretching is the secret weapon of the king of beasts. And I've made it my secret, too."

HOW STRETCHING EXERCISES HELP TODAY'S TRACK AND FIELD ATHLETES

It's been many years since Jesse Owens shared his secret with the curious young boy at the country fair. But today's track and field stars still follow his advice.

At every practice and every meet, you will see track and field athletes slowly stretching their muscles like proud young African lions. Why do they do it?

☐ Stretching loosens up tight muscles.

☐ Stretching helps the legs and arms reach farther and faster.

☐ Stretching prevents injury because it helps the muscles move farther without straining or tearing.

☐ Stretching helps condition the muscles so that an athlete can do more without getting tired.

☐ Stretching makes you a better, faster, stronger athlete.

THE RIGHT WAY TO STRETCH: LIKE A CAT

This book shows good stretching exercises for track and field events.

Stretching exercises must always be done slowly and gently like a cat.

When you're stretching, never bounce up and down. Reach very slowly and try to stretch farther and farther, a little bit at a time. When you reach a point where you begin to feel a little pain, back off very slowly.

Stretching is not a contest. You're just trying to stretch your muscles and loosen up slowly for your event. No matter what, **never bounce** and never stretch to the point of real pain.

Stretching can be done every day. But it must *always* be done before practice or meets. It's also a good idea to stretch after the event. This is called "warming down" your muscles. Doing this helps prevent stiffness or soreness.

Ready? Go to it!

9

1) THE PERISCOPE

Lie flat on your stomach with your hands to the side as if you were about to do a normal push-up. Now, slowly arch your back as shown while you raise your head as far back as possible. Hold for a few seconds.

2) SITTING BULL

Sit flat on the floor with your back placed firmly against a wall. Place the bottoms of your feet together as shown. Gently push down on the inside of both knees. Hold for a few seconds.

3) JOGGER'S STRETCH

12

Keeping both legs straight, cross your left foot over your right as shown. Slowly bend forward as far as possible. Hold for a few seconds. Repeat on other side.

14

Sit on the floor with knees bent and both feet tucked back as shown. Now, very slowly lower your back towards the floor. See if you can keep your knees from raising up. Hold the stretch for a few seconds, then rise up slowly.

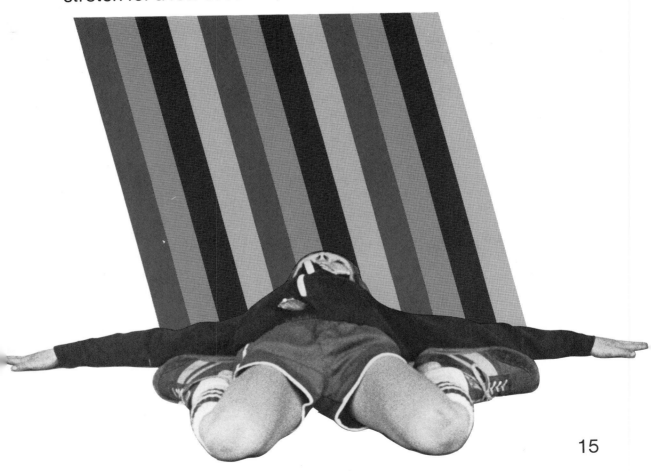

16

Lie flat on the floor with legs held high in a "V" as shown. With your hands on the inside of your knees, gently push the legs apart. Hold the stretch for a few seconds.

6) HURDLER'S STRETCH

18

Slide your left leg straight back as shown. With your palms flat on the floor for support, move your shoulders down and forward. Hold for a few seconds. Repeat on other side.

7) SITTING CRANE

Stretch your left leg straight out in front of you. Curl your right foot behind as shown. Now, slowly reach out to grab the bottom of your foot with both hands. Lower your head toward your knee. Hold for a few seconds. Repeat on the other side.

8) THE TWISTER

Sit on the floor legs pulled in and one ankle crossed over the other. Hold your arms straight out to your sides as shown. Now slowly twist your body to the left as far as it will go. Hold for a few seconds. Repeat on the other side.

21

Stand two or three feet from a wall as shown. Now, place your hands flat against the wall, and bring your left foot back as shown until the stretch is felt. Hold for a few seconds. Repeat on other side.

9) WALL STRETCH

Place the knuckles of your left hand against your upper back. Keep your elbow high against your head as shown. Now, use your right hand to gently pull the left elbow towards the middle of your back. Hold for a few seconds. Repeat on the other side.

10) WING BACKS

26

Sit flat on the floor and pull the bottoms of your feet together as shown. Now, slowly bring your forehead towards the floor. Hold for a few seconds. Repeat.

12) TOWEL STRETCH

With your hands shoulder-width apart, grasp both ends of a towel or shirt. Now, gently move your arms back behind you as far as possible until the stretch is felt. Hold for a few seconds. Repeat.

13) BOARD STRETCH

30

Place the toes of one foot on the edge of a standard two-inch by four-inch board. Now, keeping your legs straight, slowly raise your body up with the front of your foot. Hold for a few seconds. Lower and repeat.

TRACK & FIELD

THE CHILDREN'S BOOK COMPANY

FOR YOUNG PEOPLE

D1540228